HEROES FOR YOUNG READERS
ACTIVITY GUIDE
FOR BOOKS 9–12

Betty Greene • David Livingstone
Adoniram Judson • Hudson Taylor

Renee Taft Meloche

YWAM
PUBLISHING

P.O. BOX 55787 / SEATTLE, WA 98155

YWAM Publishing is the publishing ministry of Youth With A Mission. Youth With A Mission (YWAM) is an international missionary organization of Christians from many denominations dedicated to presenting Jesus Christ to this generation. To this end, YWAM has focused its efforts in three main areas: (1) training and equipping believers for their part in fulfilling the Great Commission (Matthew 28:19), (2) personal evangelism, and (3) mercy ministry (medical and relief work).

For a free catalog of books and materials, contact:

YWAM Publishing
P.O. Box 55787, Seattle, WA 98155
(425) 771-1153 or (800) 922-2143
www.ywampublishing.com

Heroes for Young Readers Activity Guide for Books 9–12
Copyright © 2005 by Renee Taft Meloche

10 09 08 07 06 05   10 9 8 7 6 5 4 3 2 1

Published by Youth With A Mission Publishing
P.O. Box 55787
Seattle, WA 98155

ISBN 1-57658-369-4 (10-digit)
ISBN 978-1-57658-369-2 (13-digit)

Printed in the United States of America.

Contents

Introduction

This activity guide is designed to accompany the following books from the Heroes for Young Readers series by Renee Taft Meloche and Bryan Pollard: *Betty Greene: Flying High*; *David Livingstone: Courageous Explorer*; *Adoniram Judson: A Grand Purpose*; and *Hudson Taylor: Friend of China*. It provides the Christian schoolteacher, Sunday-school teacher, and homeschooling parent with ways to teach and reinforce the important lessons of these books.

Each book contains the following parts:

❖ **Coloring Page.** There is a picture of each hero with memorable people and events surrounding him or her for the children to color.

❖ **Hero Song.** The hero song is a tool to reinforce the main lesson of the hero. Music is often more memorable than spoken or written text.

❖ **Character Quality.** Each hero is given a character quality for the children to focus on. Discussion questions and visual aids are provided.

❖ **Character Activity.** The character activity uses drama or arts and crafts to convey more fully the character quality of the hero.

❖ **Character Song.** The character song encourages children to develop the particular character quality in their own lives.

❖ **Shoebox Activity.** This activity uses arts and crafts to create a keepsake to remember each hero and how they served. The children will put this keepsake into a shoebox (or other container) so that they will have a treasure box of memories of the heroes.

❖ **Cultural Page.** This page illustrates something that is representative of the country each hero worked in as a missionary, such as an animal, game, craft, or recipe.

❖ **Map.** The map page, which the children will color, shows the country or countries the hero lived in growing up and as a missionary.

❖ **Flag.** A flag (usually of the country the hero worked in as a missionary) is provided for the children to color.

❖ **Fact Quiz.** This page tests the children's comprehension of each hero story by giving true and false statements inside a particular object that relates to that story. The children will color in the true statements and draw an X over the false statements.

❖ **Fun with Rhyme.** This page has five stanzas from each hero story. The last word of each stanza is blank, and the children try to fill in the blank, rhyming it with the last word in the second line. A Word Bank is provided for very young readers. (When making copies, the Word Bank can be covered up for the more advanced reader and speller.)

❖ **Crossword Puzzle.** This page tests the children's comprehension of each story. A Word Bank is provided for young readers. (Again, when making copies, the Word Bank can be covered up.)

❖ **Can You Name the Hero?** This exercise has four stanzas, each providing clues about a hero. The children guess which hero each stanza is about.

Before you begin this activity guide, you may want to highlight which activities best suit your needs. For instance, a Sunday-school teacher might want to focus on the coloring pages, songs, character activities, and shoebox activities, while a schoolteacher might want to focus more on the crossword puzzle, fact, map, and cultural pages. A thirteen-week syllabus is included at the end of this activity guide for those parents and teachers who would like a guide to covering some or all of the activities.

Reinforcing stories with fun and creative illustrations, songs, drama, and arts and crafts brings the heroes to life and helps the children remember the important lessons learned through the lives of heroes—ordinary men and women who did extraordinary things with God.

Betty Greene: Flying High

Betty Greene Song

Betty Greene became a pilot, for she loved to fly. The view above was heavenly, way up there in the sky.

She earned silver wings and joined a flying ministry, and found how helpful even just one single plane can be.

The lifeline, the lifeline, her airplane was a lifeline, improving missionaries' lives who needed her supplies.

The lifeline, the lifeline, her airplane was a lifeline. Betty served the Lord in flight and was a welcome sight.

The Good Character Quality
of Betty Greene

SERVICE

Definition of Service: Helping others and meeting their needs.

Bible Verse: "Serve wholeheartedly, as if you were serving the Lord, not men, because you know that the Lord will reward everyone for whatever good he does" (Ephesians 6:7–8).

Materials

❖ Copy of the crown, strip, and diamond jewel labeled "service" on page 12 for each child (use heavy white paper or card stock; if you do not wish to have the children color their crowns, use heavy yellow paper or yellow card stock)
❖ Scissors
❖ Crayons or colored pencils
❖ Stapler
❖ Tape or glue

Steps to Follow

1. Introduce the character quality of service, which describes Betty, and discuss its meaning with the children. Read aloud the Bible verse above.

2. Have the children color and cut out the diamond labeled "service." (Because it is a diamond, tell them they may want to leave the middle part white.)

3. Have the children color and cut out their crown and strip. Read aloud the following Bible verse: "Now there is in store for me the crown of righteousness, which the Lord, the righteous Judge, will award to me on that day" (2 Timothy 4:8).

4. Have the children tape or glue the diamond to their crown. Then have them staple the strip to the crown and put it around their heads. This will serve as their "thinking cap" about service.

5. Ask the children, "How did Betty serve through her actions?"
   ❖ She served her country during World War Two, flying planes and testing new equipment, even though it was dangerous.

❖ She served the missionaries by flying them to different places.

❖ She brought the missionaries food, mail, and medical supplies to use themselves and to distribute to those they served.

6. Ask the children if they know someone—a parent, a neighbor, or friend—who demonstrates service in their life. Have them tell the class about this person.

7. Have the children sing the character song "We'll Try Hard to Serve" on page 13. (This song is sung to the tune of "Do Your Ears Hang Low?" If you have the CD for Betty Greene, you can have the children follow or sing along with this song. At the end of the CD, there is a solo piano accompaniment, which the children can sing along with as well.)

Note: This activity carries over into all the hero stories that follow. For each hero, there will be a new character quality inside a different jewel. You can have the children keep adding jewels to the crowns that they've already made or have them make new crowns each time this activity is repeated. Please be aware that the jewels are a fun way to reinforce the lesson, not a suggestion that the children should expect to be rewarded for doing the right thing as Christians.

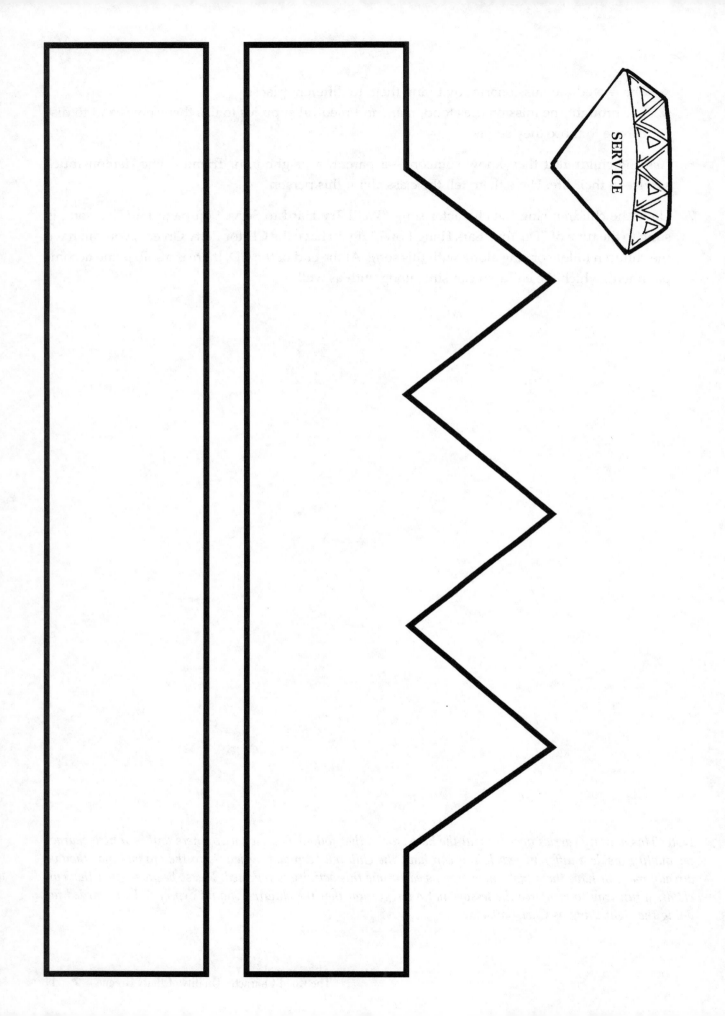

Betty Greene Character Song

We'll Try Hard to Serve

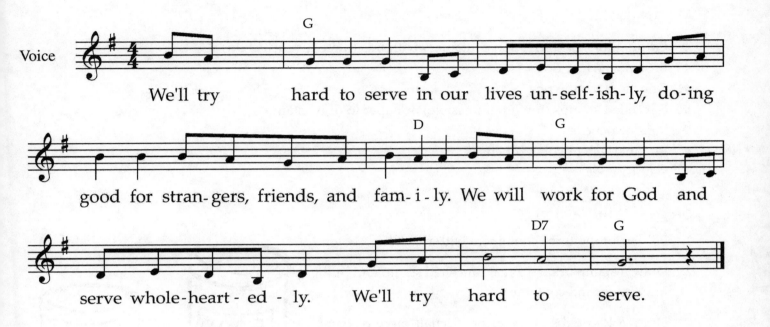

We'll try hard to serve in our lives un-self-ish-ly, do-ing good for stran-gers, friends, and fam-i-ly. We will work for God and serve whole-heart-ed-ly. We'll try hard to serve.

Character Activity for Betty Greene

Showing Ways to Serve

Materials

- ❖ Empty film or prescription containers with lids (three for each child)
- ❖ Brown or white rice
- ❖ One bowl for the rice
- ❖ Cancelled stamps (foreign if possible) or paper to draw stamps
- ❖ Pens or pencils
- ❖ Red markers or colored pencils
- ❖ White paper

Steps to Follow

1. Fill one of the three containers with rice from a bowl.

2. Draw a stamp or take a real cancelled stamp and put it into the second container.

3. Draw a Red Cross symbol on a small piece of paper and put it into the third container.

4. On a piece of paper, write the word *Food* (small enough to tape to the outside of the container). Cut out the word and tape it to the container holding the rice.

5. Write the word *Mail*, cut it out, and tape it to the container with the stamp.

6. Write the word *Medical*, cut it out, and tape it to the container with the Red Cross.

7. Have the children put the lids on each one of their containers and tell them that these were three ways that Betty helped to serve missionaries and others around the world.

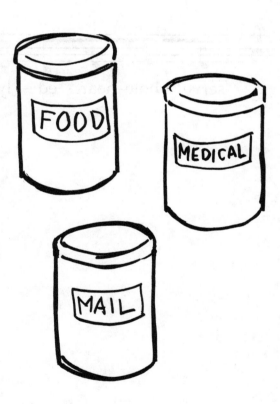

Shoebox Activity for Betty Greene
Making Airplanes

Note to parents and teachers: A Shoebox Activity is included for each Christian hero in this activity guide. At the end of each missionary adventure that the children experience, the children will have keepsakes to put in their shoeboxes of memories. If you prefer, you may choose a different container in which the children can store their keepsakes.

Materials

- ❖ Two Life Savers for each child
- ❖ One long piece of hard candy for each child (a roll of wrapped Smarties, a long Tootsie Roll, or a small candy cane with the top broken off)
- ❖ One stick of gum for each child
- ❖ One medium-size rubber band for each child

Steps to Follow

1. Put the rubber band through both Life Savers.

2. Place the piece of candy between the two Life Savers and on top of the rubber band.

3. Place the stick of gum across the Life Savers and hard candy and loop the rubber band ends over the ends of the stick of gum, holding the gum in place.

4. Have the children put their airplanes in their shoeboxes. This will help to remind them of how God led Betty on her many journeys in flight.

Caution: Some children, because of health reasons, should not be given candy. Please take all necessary precautions, including asking each child's parent or guardian for permission to give the child candy.

Note: If the children wish to take their airplanes home right away, have them make an extra one for their shoeboxes.

Echidna Spiny Anteater of New Guinea

The echidna has tiny eyes, short legs with sharp claws on its feet, tough spines covering the top of its body, a pointy snout, and a tiny mouth. Although the echidna has no teeth, it has a long, sticky tongue, which it uses to catch insects.

The echidnas lay a single egg, which hatches in ten days, in a pouch on the female's belly. The blind and hairless baby echidna gets milk from a gland within the mother's pouch. In a few weeks, the baby echidna (called a puggle) develops sharp spines and must leave the pouch.

The echidna can live for over fifty years, and when attacked it will quickly burrow in the ground or curl up in a ball.

The echidna has a black to brown coat. Color the echidna below.

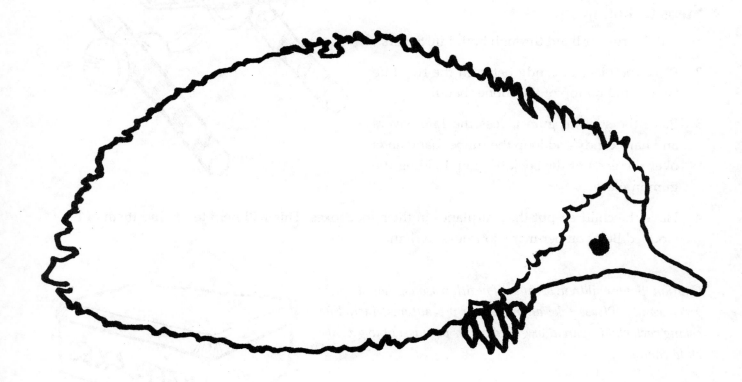

Map: Betty Greene

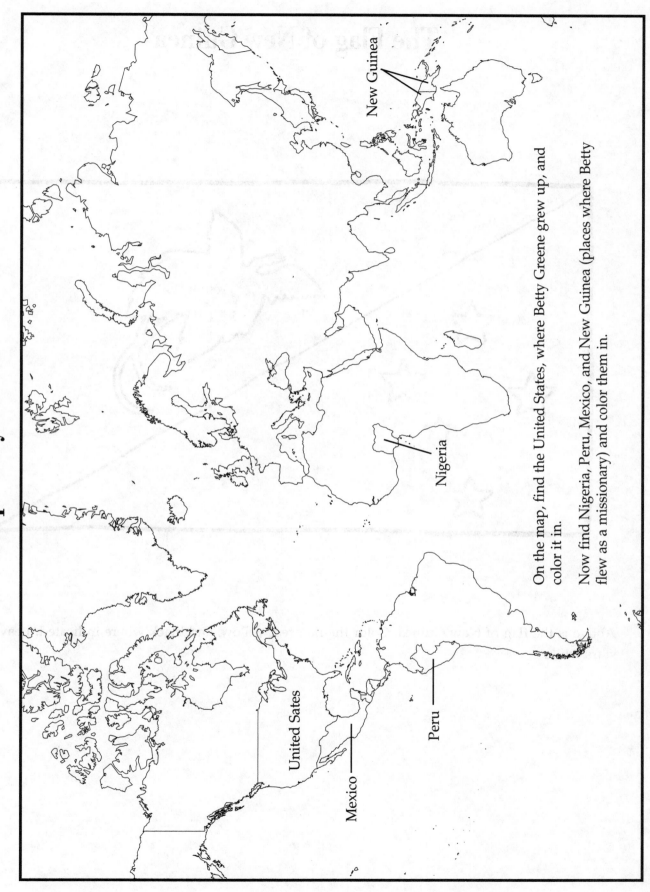

New Guinea

Nigeria

United Sates

Mexico

Peru

On the map, find the United States, where Betty Greene grew up, and color it in.

Now find Nigeria, Peru, Mexico, and New Guinea (places where Betty flew as a missionary) and color them in.

The Flag of New Guinea

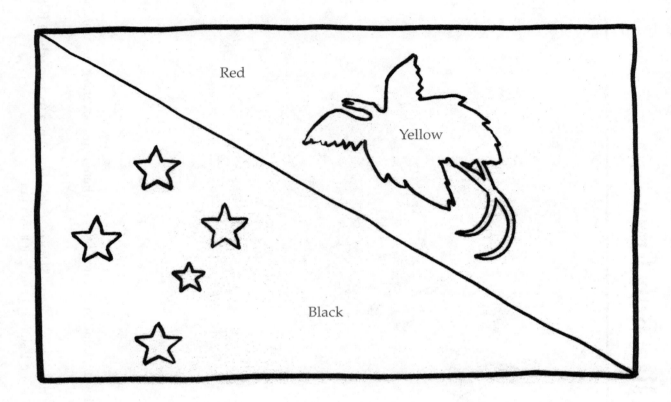

Red

Yellow

Black

Above is the flag of New Guinea. Color the flag red, yellow, and black where indicated. Leave the stars white.

Betty Greene Quiz

Color the airplanes whose facts are correct.
Draw a big X over the airplanes whose facts are incorrect.

Betty learned how to fly a large float plane near her home.

Betty performed very safe flying tests during World War II.

Betty started a flying ministry after the war.

Betty delivered food, mail, and medical supplies to the missionaries.

Betty flew a red biplane into Mexico.

Betty flew into a severe rainstorm in Nigeria.

Betty flew to an unexplored island called New Guinea.

Betty took an easy, relaxing hike to inspect an airstrip in New Guinea.

Airplanes are rarely used today to help missionaries.

God wants us to use our gifts for Him.

Fun with Rhyme

It's your turn to be a poet. See if you can fill in the correct word inside each airplane without looking at your book on Betty Greene. Hint: The word will rhyme with the last word in the second line.

Word Bank

face

dream

sight

best

day

In nineteen forty-one, a tall
    young woman, Betty Greene,
became a pilot, something that
    had been her childhood

Though Betty knew how dangerous
    it was to do these tests,
her flying skills had proved to be
    among her unit's

The pilots would help missionaries
    get from place to place,
and help them with emergencies
    they frequently would

Then after news was sent out that
    the airstrip was okay,
a humming sound grew louder in
    the forest that same

If we can use our gifts for God
    as Betty did, in flight,
then like her plane, we too can be
    a helpful, welcome

Betty Greene Crossword Puzzle

Word Bank

Peru

camel

fly

Washington

Mexico

sight

Two

Cessna

dune

Nigeria

Across

3. Country in South America where Betty flew.
6. American state where Betty grew up.
7. Something Betty loved to do.
8. Type of plane that landed in New Guinea.
10. Betty flew planes during World War _ _ _.

Down

1. Country that borders America where Betty flew.
2. A ridge or hill of wind-blown sand.
4. A humped long-necked mammal in Africa.
5. Country in Africa where Betty flew.
9. Betty's plane was a helpful, welcome _ _ _ _ _.

David Livingstone: Courageous Explorer

David Livingstone Song

David was a doctor who knew science very well. He went to Africa to treat the people who were ill.

In this land of drums and lions, he was not afraid. Even when a lion shook him, he was very brave.

A doctor, a doctor, David was a doctor. He healed a chief and his sick son and other Africans.

A doctor, a doctor, David was a doctor. In unexplored and tribal land, David was God's hands.

The Good Character Quality
of David Livingstone

Definition of Boldness: Being willing to undertake things that involve risk or danger.

Bible Verse: "When I called, you answered me; you made me bold and stouthearted" (Psalm 138:3).

Materials

- ❖ Copy of the crown, strip, and emerald jewel labeled "boldness" on page 28 for each child (use heavy white paper or card stock; if you do not wish to have the children color their crowns, use heavy yellow paper or yellow card stock)
- ❖ Scissors
- ❖ Crayons or colored pencils
- ❖ Stapler
- ❖ Tape or glue

Steps to Follow

1. Introduce the character quality of boldness, which describes David, and discuss its meaning with the children. Read aloud the Bible verse above.

2. Have the children color and cut out the emerald labeled "boldness." (Because it is an emerald, you may want to suggest they color it green.)

3. Have the children color and cut out the crown and strip. Read aloud the following Bible verse: "Be faithful … and I will give you the crown of life" (Rev. 2:10).

4. Have the children tape or glue the emerald to the crown. Then have them staple the strip to the crown and put it around their heads. This will serve as their "thinking cap" about boldness.

5. Ask the children, "How did David show boldness through his words and actions?"
   - ❖ David boldly ventured inland into Africa where no white man had gone before.
   - ❖ David boldly treated anyone who was sick, including the chief with damaged eyes.
   - ❖ David boldly stepped between the warrior and the eleven-year-old girl who was to be married.

❖ David boldly searched for the lion that had been killing sheep.

❖ David boldly shared stories from the Bible with the Africans.

6. Ask the children if they know someone—a parent, neighbor, or friend—who shows boldness in their life. Have them tell the class about this person.

7. Have the children sing the character song "We Will Be So Bold" on page 29. (This song is sung to the tune of "Do Your Ears Hang Low?" If you have the CD for David Livingstone, you can have the children follow or sing along with this song. At the end of the CD, there is a solo piano accompaniment, which the children can sing along with as well.)

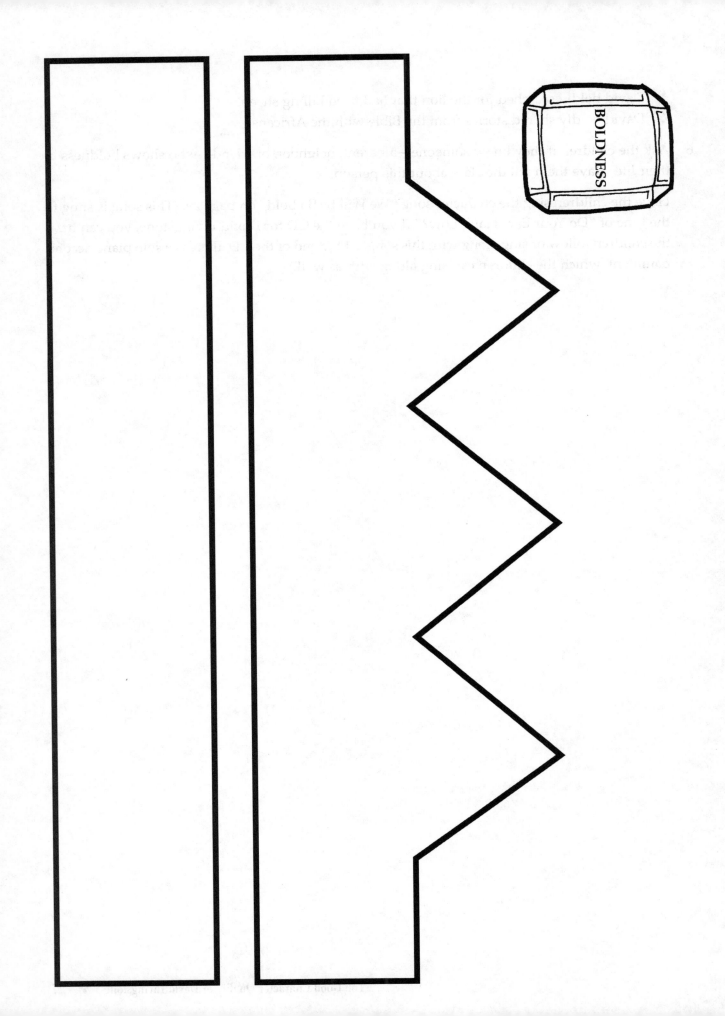

BOLDNESS

David Livingstone Character Song

We Will Be So Bold

Character Activity for David Livingstone

Going on a Lion Hunt

Note: You can have the children follow along on the companion CD for books 9–12 (track number 11) or you can lead the children yourself, following the steps below.

Steps to Follow

1. Tell the children, "David Livingstone showed great boldness in his life, and he bravely searched for the lion that had been killing sheep. We're going to go on a lion hunt and show how bold we can be."

2. "When we shut the door, we'll clap." (Clap.)

3. "When we march, we'll slap our thighs." (Slap your thighs at a fast, steady rhythm.)

4. "When we go over the bridge, we'll slap our upper chest with open palms." (Slap your upper chest with open palms.)

5. "When we go through the stream, we'll rub our palms together." (Rub your palms together.)

6. "When we jump the chasm, we'll jump like a rabbit without leaving our seats." (Jump like a rabbit without leaving your seat.)

7. "When we look for lions, we will look left and then ahead and then right with our hands shading our eyes." (Look left, then ahead, then right, with your hand shading your eyes.)

8. "Okay, kids, this is serious business, so are you ready?"

9. "Say goodbye to mama." (Pat hand lightly over mouth several times and make a whooping sound.)

10. "Shut the door." (Clap.)

11. "On the road." (Slap your thighs at a fast, steady rhythm.)

12. "Over the bridge." (Slap your upper chest with open palms.)

13. "Back on the road." (Slap your thighs at a fast, steady rhythm.)

14. "Through the stream." (Rub your palms together.)

15. "Back on the road." (Slap your thighs at a fast, steady rhythm.)

16. "Over the chasm." (Jump like a rabbit without leaving your seat.)

17. "Back on the road." (Slap your thighs at a fast, steady rhythm.)

18. "Up the hill." (Slap your thighs at a slow, steady rhythm.) "We're not afraid of those lions. They're nothing but big, overgrown pussycats."

19. "Stop. Look for lions." (Look left, then ahead, and then right with your hand shading your eyes.) "No lions to the left. No lions straight ahead. No lions to the right."

20. "Back up the hill." (Slap your thighs at a slow steady rhythm.) "We have no fear of those lions."

21. "Stop. Look for lions. No lions to the left." (Look left with your hand shading your eyes, then start to look straight ahead.)

22. "There's a lion!" (Shout this loudly.)

23. "Down the hill!" (Slap your thighs at a furious pace.)

24. "Over the chasm." (Jump like a rabbit without leaving your seat at a furious pace.)

25. "Back on the road." (Slap your thighs at a furious pace.)

26. "Through the stream." (Rub your palms together.)

27. "Back on the road." (Slap your thighs at a furious pace.)

28. "Over the bridge." (Slap your upper chest with open palms at a furious pace.)

29. "Back on the road." (Slap your thighs at a furious pace.)

30. (Clap as if shutting the door, then give a whooping sound to say hello to mama.)

31. Explain to the children: "The Bible says, 'When I called, you answered me; you made me bold.' Only with God's help can we show real boldness in our lives."

Shoebox Activity for David Livingstone

Making a Doctor's Bag

Materials

- ❖ Small ziplock bags (one for each child)
- ❖ Permanent markers
- ❖ Masking tape
- ❖ Medical supplies (you can add or substitute others):
  - ✓ Band-Aids
  - ✓ Cotton balls
  - ✓ Cotton swabs
  - ✓ Tongue depressors

Steps to Follow

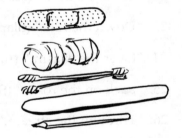

1. Have the children take a ziplock bag and fill it with two or three each of medical supplies, such as Band-Aids, cotton balls, cotton swabs, and tongue depressors.

2. Have the children write their own title or name, such as "Dr. Daniel" or "Dr. Thompson," on a piece of masking tape and tape it to the outside of the ziplock bag containing all of their supplies.

3. Have the children put their doctor's bag in their shoeboxes with all their other keepsakes. This will help remind them of how David shared God's love in Africa as he healed the sick.

Africa's Lions

Lions are large, meat-eating mammals. They are light brown to brownish orange in color. The male has a thick, full-flowing mane. Lions are very large and can weigh as much as 600 pounds.

Materials

- ❖ Copy of the lion pattern (on the following page) on yellow card stock (one for each child)
- ❖ One dozen 1.25 x 8.5 inch orange paper strips (for each child)
- ❖ Six thin, brown paper strips for whiskers (for each child)
- ❖ Crayons or colored pencils
- ❖ Scissors
- ❖ Glue
- ❖ Stapler

Steps to Follow

1. Give one copy of the lion pattern to each child.

2. Have the children color the lion's eyes, nose, and ears.

3. Cut out the pattern.

4. Glue on strips of brown paper for the lion's whiskers.

5. Glue, staple, or tape the ends of each orange paper strip together, without creasing the strip, forming a loop.

6. Glue, staple, or tape the closed ends of the paper loops around the back top and sides of the lion's head to make the lion's mane.

Map: David Livingstone

On the map, find the country of Scotland, where David Livingstone grew up, and color it in.

Now find the continent of Africa, where David lived and traveled as a missionary, and color it in.

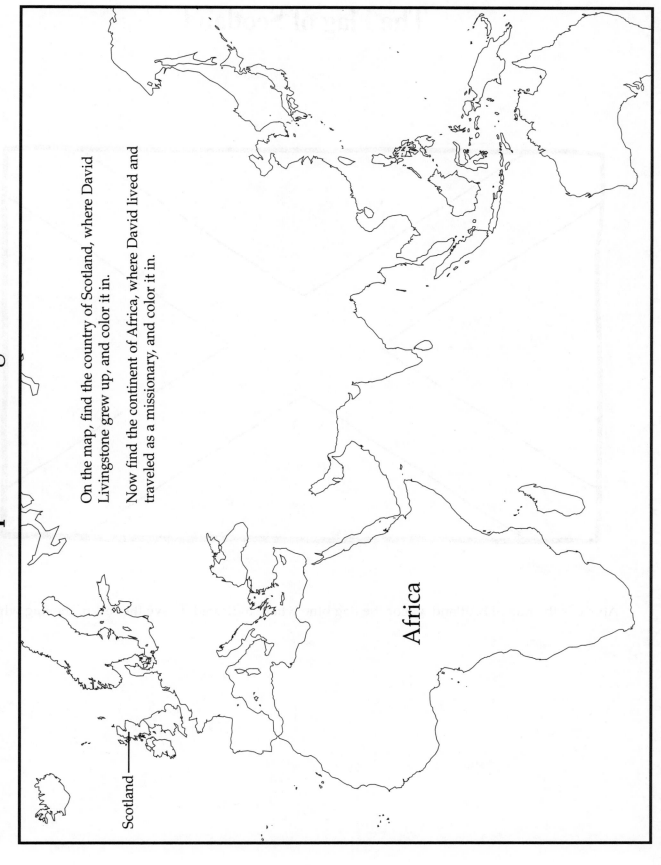

Scotland

Africa

The Flag of Scotland

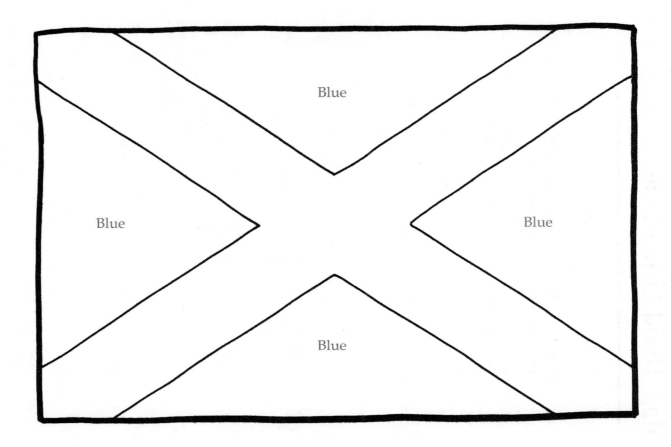

Above is the flag of Scotland. Color the flag blue where indicated. Leave the rest of the flag white.

David Livingstone Quiz

Color the lions whose facts are correct.
Draw a big X over the lions whose facts are incorrect.

David worked in a cotton mill when he was twelve years old.

David's father encouraged him to read science books.

David became a doctor because they were needed overseas.

David gave the chief a Bible, and he later became a Christian.

David never left the coast of Africa.

The Africans lived in round huts with roofs of straw.

David encouraged the Africans to talk about their beliefs.

David never learned what plants and fruits to eat in Africa.

David helped heal a chief whose eyes were damaged.

David tried to help the chief's sick son but failed.

Fun with Rhyme

It's your turn to be a poet. See if you can fill in the correct word inside each lion without looking at your book on David Livingstone. Hint: The word rhymes with the last word in the second line.

Word Bank

well

ground

lands

pants

day

His precious book was hidden—
   a science book on plants.
He felt it tied against his legs
   inside his trouser _____

To be a doctor seemed so right
   when he went home to pray,
and David's father changed his view
   of science that same _____

The next day, David got his bag
   and told his guide to tell
the sick to come, and he would do
   his best to make them _____

It was a little farther on
   when David heard the sound
of someone sobbing underneath
   his wagon, near the _____

Like David, with his science skills,
   we too can be God's hands,
with any special skills we have,
   in any of God's _____

David Livingstone Crossword Puzzle

Word Bank

Scotland

science

doctor

forty

chief

lion

warrior

hands

ointment

Africa

Across

1. We too can be God's _ _ _ _ _.
3. An African man who goes to battle.
6. The continent where David worked as a missionary.
8. The animal that attacked David.
9. Type of books David was forbidden to read.
10. What David studied to become.

Down

2. Country in Great Britain where David grew up.
4. David traveled _ _ _ _ _ thousand miles in Africa.
5. Kind of medicine David put on the chief's eyes.
7. The person who rules a tribe.

Adoniram Judson Song

In Burma, Adoniram preached to those from far and wide. The king threw him in prison though; he thought he was a spy.

So Adoniram went to jail, but hidden secretly inside a pillow was God's Word translated in Burmese.

In Burma, in Burma, he hid the Word in Burma. When Adoniram was set free, he shared it eagerly.

In Burma, in Burma, he hid the Word in Burma. Today in Burma, God's own Word is spread and told and heard.

The Good Character Quality
of Adoniram Judson

Definition of Purposeful: Having meaning in one's life through having a goal.

Bible Verse: "We constantly pray for you, that our God may count you worthy of his calling, and that by his power he may fulfill every good purpose of yours" (2 Thessalonians 1:11).

Materials

- ❖ Copy of the crown, strip, and ruby jewel labeled "purposeful" on page 46 for each child (use heavy white paper or card stock; if you do not wish to have the children color their crowns, use heavy yellow paper or yellow card stock)
- ❖ Scissors
- ❖ Crayons or colored pencils
- ❖ Stapler
- ❖ Tape or glue

Steps to Follow

1. Introduce the character quality of purposefulness, which describes Adoniram, and discuss its meaning with the children. Read aloud the Bible verse above.

2. Have the children color and cut out the ruby labeled "purposeful." (Because it is a ruby, tell them they may want to color it red.)

3. Have the children color and cut out their crown and strip. Read aloud the following Bible verse: "Do you not know that in a race all the runners run, but only one gets the prize? Run in such a way as to get the prize. Everyone who competes in the games goes into strict training. They do it to get a crown that will not last; but we do it to get a crown that will last forever" (1 Corinthians 9:24–25).

4. Have the children tape or glue the ruby to the crown. Then have them staple the strip to the crown and put it around their heads. This will serve as their "thinking cap" about being purposeful.

5. Ask the children: "What was Adoniram's purpose when he first got out of college?"
   ❖ To search for greatness, riches, and reward.

6. "Did this purpose make him happy?"
   ❖ No.

7. "After Adoniram studied the Bible and finally believed it was true, what became his purpose then?"
   ❖ To live his life for God and others; to go to Burma and share God's love with the Burmese people.

8. Ask the children if they know someone—a parent, neighbor, or friend—who demonstrates purposefulness in their life. Have them tell the class about this person.

9. Have the children sing the character song "We'll Be Purposeful" on page 47. (This song is sung to the tune of "Do Your Ears Hang Low?" If you have the CD for Adoniram Judson, you can have the children follow or sing along with this song. At the end of the CD, there is a solo piano accompaniment, which the children can sing along with as well.)

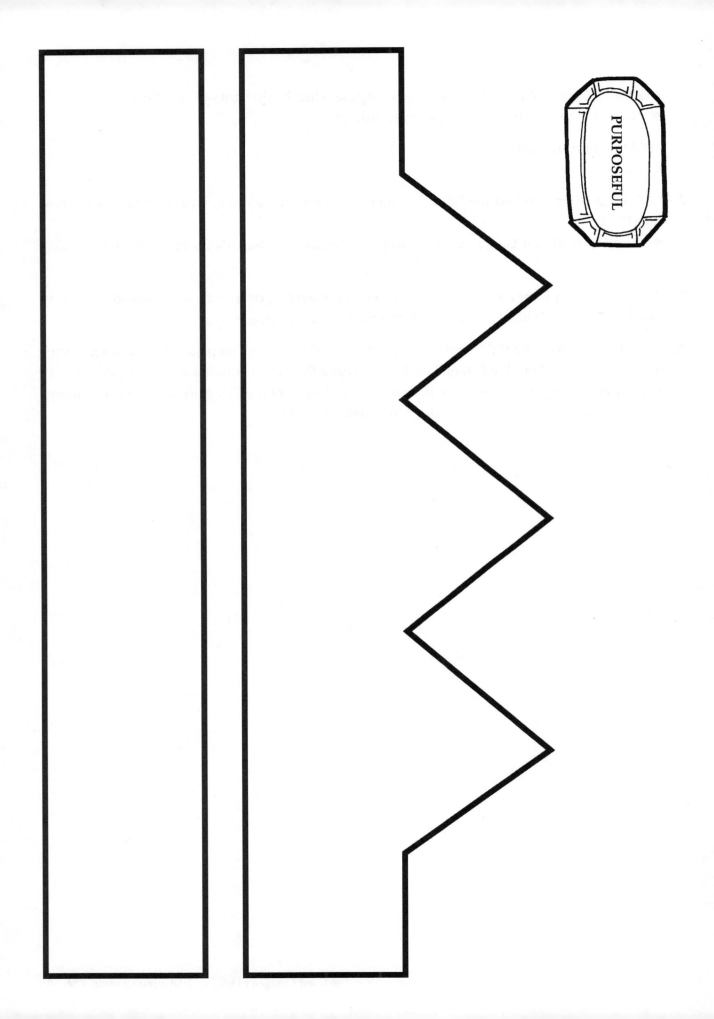

PURPOSEFUL

Adoniram Judson Character Song

We'll Be Purposeful

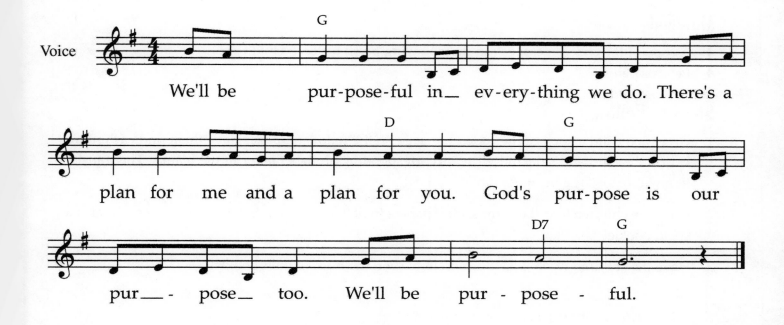

Character Activity for Adoniram Judson

Translating the Bible

Materials

- ❖ A copy of the coded message (on the following page) for each child
- ❖ Pens or pencils

Steps to Follow

1. Give each child a copy of the coded message on the following page. Have them find each number on the left-hand side and write its corresponding alphabet letter in the blanks. The translation will read: "The Burmese Bible."

2. Have the children fold their translation papers in half and then in half two more times to form a small booklet.

3. Have the children write "The Burmese Bible" on the front of their booklets.

Note: This activity carries over into the Shoebox Activity.

Translate the Code

8 2 1   0 9 6 5 1 7 1   0 3 0 4 1

___ _____ _____

Now it's your turn to be a translator like Adoniram Judson. Figure out the message above by matching each number with the alphabet letter on its right and write it in the space provided. For example, the first number above is 8. In the chart below, 8 equals (or becomes) a T. Write T in the blank under 8.

0 = B	5 = M
1 = E	6 = R
2 = H	7 = S
3 = I	8 = T
4 = L	9 = U

Shoebox Activity for Adoniram Judson

Keeping the Bible Safe

Materials

- ❖ Stapler
- ❖ Scissors
- ❖ Thick, white paper
- ❖ Polyester fiberfill

Steps to Follow

1. Take a piece of thick, white paper (to represent a pillow), fold it once widthwise, and then staple the side and one end shut, leaving one end open.

2. Slide the translated "Burmese Bibles" (see Character Activity on pages 48 and 49) into the pillow through the open side.

3. Stuff some polyester fiberfill into the "pillow" and staple the last side shut.

4. Have the children put their pillows inside their shoeboxes with all their other keepsakes. This will remind them of the important work Adoniram did in translating the Bible into Burmese.

The Bengal Tiger of Burma

The Bengal tiger is a large, striped cat that lives in tropical jungle, brush, and tall grasslands. The Bengal tiger lives in Burma as well as in the countries of India, Nepal, and Bhutan.

The male Bengal tiger weighs about 500 pounds and the female 300 pounds. The Bengal tiger is a carnivore (meat eater) and can eat as much as eighty-eight pounds of meat in one feeding. They have long, sharp teeth and powerful jaws and often kill their prey with a bite on the neck. They eat deer, pigs, antelope, cattle, young elephants, and buffalo. They hunt mostly at dusk, and their dark stripes help them hide in the shadows of tall grasses. Since they are not able to chase their prey for a long distance, they often stalk and pounce on their prey instead. They often drag their prey to water to eat. When they have eaten their fill, the leftovers become food for a variety of mammals, birds, and reptiles.

The Bengal tiger lives about fifteen years in the wild. Due to over-hunting, these tigers are in danger of extinction. Fewer than 3,000 Bengal tigers exist in the wild today.

The Bengal tiger has a long tail, long legs, and sharp claws. They are usually orange-brown in color with black stripes.

Color the Bengal tiger on the following page.

The Bengal Tiger

Map: Adoniram Judson

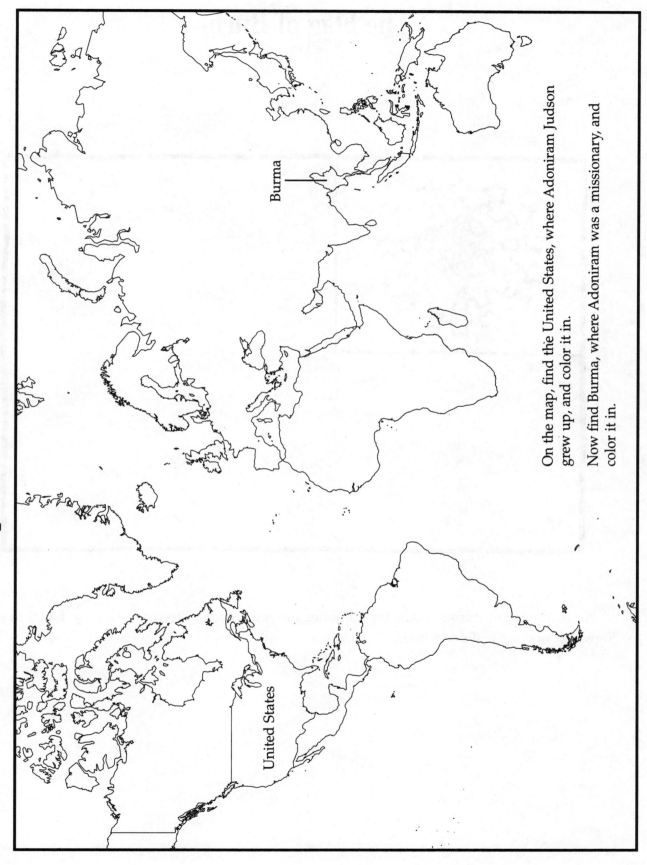

Burma

United States

On the map, find the United States, where Adoniram Judson grew up, and color it in.

Now find Burma, where Adoniram was a missionary, and color it in.

The Flag of Burma

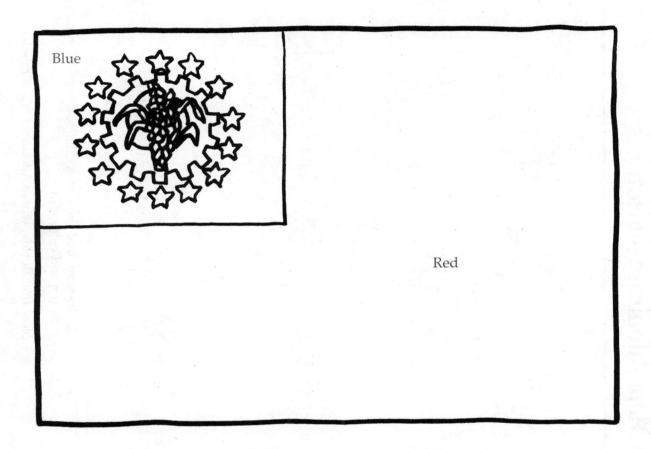

Above is the flag of Burma. Color the flag blue and red where indicated. Leave the fourteen stars, cogwheel, and stalk of rice white.

Adoniram Judson Quiz

Color the pillows whose facts are correct.
Draw a big X over the pillows whose facts are incorrect.

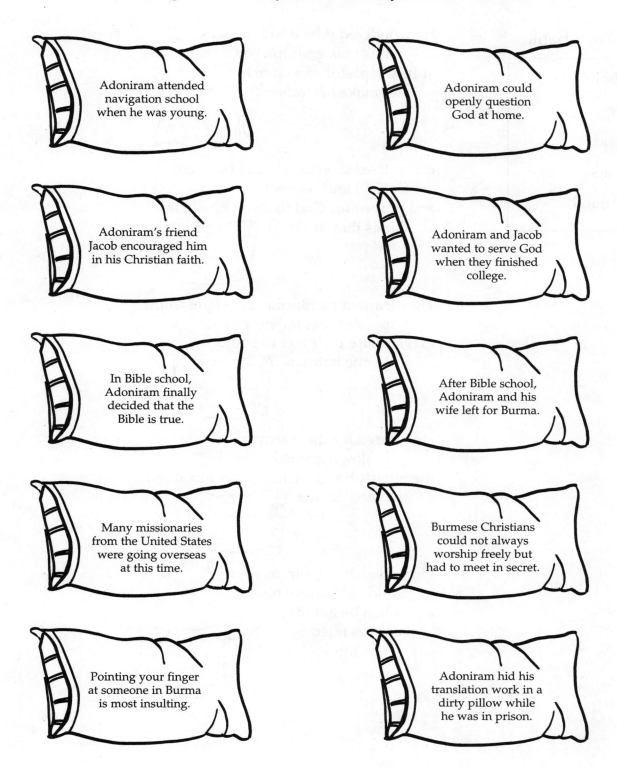

Adoniram attended navigation school when he was young.

Adoniram could openly question God at home.

Adoniram's friend Jacob encouraged him in his Christian faith.

Adoniram and Jacob wanted to serve God when they finished college.

In Bible school, Adoniram finally decided that the Bible is true.

After Bible school, Adoniram and his wife left for Burma.

Many missionaries from the United States were going overseas at this time.

Burmese Christians could not always worship freely but had to meet in secret.

Pointing your finger at someone in Burma is most insulting.

Adoniram hid his translation work in a dirty pillow while he was in prison.

Fun with Rhyme

It's your turn to be a poet. See if you can fill in the correct word inside each pillow without looking at your book on Adoniram Judson. Hint: The word rhymes with the last word in the second line.

Word Bank

show

do

glad

tears

ground

He wondered if he'd sail the seas
   just like his grandpa had,
or be the pastor of a church
   and make his father ___

He realized then life should be lived
   for God and others too,
and prayed for God to show him helpful
   things that he could ___

They learned the Burmese customs; most
   important was to know
to never use their feet to point
   or let the bottoms ___

He headed for the courtyard and
   then slowly turned around:
the guards had smashed his bamboo hut
   to pieces on the ___

He smiled at Adoniram who
   could not believe his ears,
and when he got his pages back
   his eyes filled up with ___

Adoniram Judson Crossword Puzzle

Word Bank

spies

pillow

banyan

Burma

elephant

stamp

Massachusetts

Burmese

Britain

bamboo

Across

1. Adoniram translated the Bible into this language.
3. Country Adoniram served in as a missionary.
4. Place Adoniram hid his translation work.
5. Country that invaded Burma.
7. Name of the state where Adoniram grew up.

Down

1. What Adoniram's prison hut was made of.
2. An animal they rode in Burma.
6. Type of tree in Burma.
8. The king felt all foreigners were _ _ _ _ _.
9. One must never point or _ _ _ _ _ the feet.

Hudson Taylor: Friend of China

Hudson Taylor Song

A man named Hudson Taylor prayed and knew it was God's plan for him to go to China, to that ancient, distant land.

Since he was told his blue eyes and blond hair would never do, he wore a false pig-tail, and on his feet were curled-up shoes.

The mission, the mission, the China Inland Mission. In the land of panda bears, the mission gave out care.

The mission, the mission, the China Inland Mission. Hudson and his team showed love for our great God above.

The Good Character Quality
of Hudson Taylor

Definition of Leadership: The ability to inspire and lead.

Bible Verse: "The Lord has sought out a man after his own heart and appointed him leader of his people" (1 Samuel 13:14).

Materials

* Copy of the crown, strip, and opal jewel labeled "leadership" on page 64 for each child (use heavy white paper or card stock; if you do not wish to have the children color their crowns, use heavy yellow paper or yellow card stock)
* Scissors
* Crayons or colored pencils
* Stapler
* Tape or glue

Steps to Follow

1. Introduce the character quality of leadership, which describes Hudson, and discuss its meaning with the children. Read aloud the Bible verse above.

2. Have the children color and cut out the opal labeled "leadership." (Because it is an opal, tell them they may want to color it milky white or pastel.)

3. Have the children color and cut out the crown and strip. Read aloud the following Bible verse: "And when the Chief Shepherd appears, you will receive the crown of glory that will never fade away" (1 Peter 5:4).

4. Have the children tape or glue the opal to the crown. Then have them staple the strip to the crown and put it around their heads. This will serve as their "thinking cap" about leadership.

5. Ask the children, "How did Hudson show leadership through his words and actions?"
   * He started the China Inland Mission and inspired many throughout the world, as well as Chinese Christians, to join him.

- ❖ He dressed and wore his hair like the Chinese and encouraged his men to do the same.
- ❖ Hudson served the Chinese as a physician, which was a wonderful example to them and to the men and women of his mission.
- ❖ Hudson's Chinese speech and manners toward the Chinese showed good leadership qualities that the men and women of his mission tried to imitate.
- ❖ When Hudson and his team were being threatened by a mob in Yangchow, Hudson showed good judgment and quick thinking as a leader by running to get help from the mandarin.

6. Ask the children if they know someone—a parent, neighbor, or friend—who demonstrates leadership in their life. Have them tell the class about this person.

7. Have the children sing the character song "We'll Work Hard to Lead" on page 65. (This song is sung to the tune of "Do Your Ears Hang Low?" If you have the CD for Hudson Taylor, you can have the children follow or sing along with this song. At the end of the CD, there is a solo piano accompaniment, which the children can sing along with as well.)

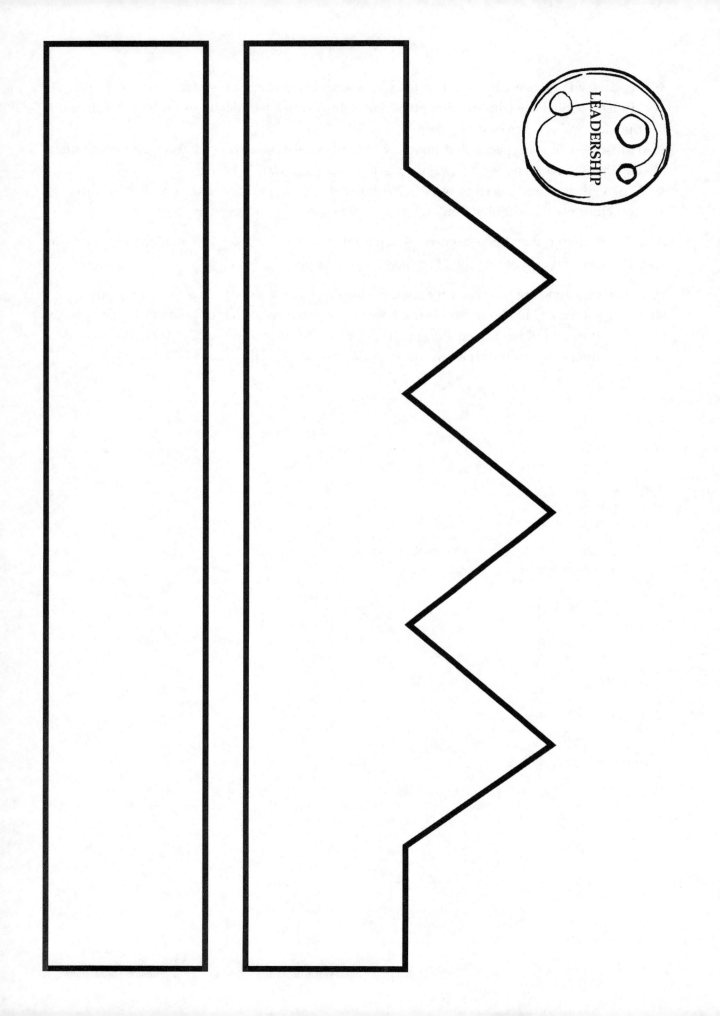

LEADERSHIP

Hudson Taylor Character Song

We'll Work Hard to Lead

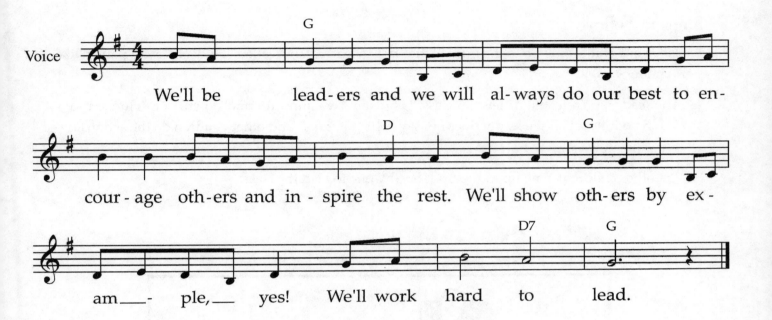

We'll be lead-ers and we will al-ways do our best to en-

cour-age oth-ers and in-spire the rest. We'll show oth-ers by ex-

am___-ple,___ yes! We'll work hard to lead.

Character Activity for Hudson Taylor

Showing Leadership

Steps to Follow

1. Have one child come up to the front of the class to lead a game called "Hudson Says," played like "Simon Says."

2. The leader in front might tell the class, "Hudson says jump up and down," or "Hudson says touch your head." If the leader does not say "Hudson says" and other children do the action anyway, they must sit down.

3. Let other children come up to the front one by one to lead the class.

Shoebox Activity for Hudson Taylor
Teamwork

Demonstrating Teamwork

Steps to Follow

1. Group the children into twos, threes, or fours.

2. Tell them they must demonstrate, using their bodies, the working action(s) of a machine, such as a washing machine, vacuum cleaner, sewing machine, typewriter, or copy machine.

3. Have each group perform their action in front of the class, and have the class guess what the machine is.

4. Then have the groups make up imaginary factory machines.

4. Have the children demonstrate the imaginary machines and explain what the machines do.

Drawing Teamwork Pictures

Materials

- ❖ Colored pencils or crayons
- ❖ Plain white paper

Steps to Follow

1. Have the children draw a picture showing two or more people demonstrating teamwork. For example:
   - ❖ Building a fire together
   - ❖ Putting up a tent
   - ❖ Helping others by passing out food, medicine, and clothes
   - ❖ Playing a game using teamwork

2. Have the children put their pictures inside their shoe-boxes with all their other keepsakes. This will remind them of the important work Hudson did with his team in China.

Chinese Lantern

Paper and cloth lanterns are often used as decorations inside Chinese homes or at the front door during weddings, festivals, and other special occasions. The lantern's frame is made of bamboo strips or metal wire and colorful paper or cloth. Traditional lanterns are shaped like giant red balls, but others are shaped like airplanes, birds, dragons, rabbits, and other interesting things.

Materials

- ❖ 8.5 x 11 inch piece of colored paper (one sheet for each child)
- ❖ Scissors
- ❖ Glue, tape, or a stapler
- ❖ Strips of colored construction paper or gift wrapping paper

Steps to Follow

1. Fold the paper lengthwise, making a long rectangle.

2. Make at least a dozen cuts along the fold line. Do not to cut all the way to the edge of the paper; leave at least a half inch.

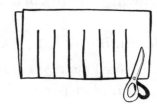

3. Unfold the paper, form it into a circle with the folded edges pointing outward, and tape or staple it closed.

4. Have the children cut a strip of paper six inches long and a half inch wide. Glue or staple this strip of paper across one end of the lantern to make a handle.

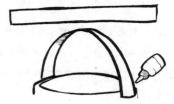

Map: Hudson Taylor

On the map, find England, where Hudson Taylor grew up, and color it in.

Now find China, where Hudson lived as a missionary, and color it in.

England

China

The Flag of China

Above is the flag of China. Color the stars yellow and the rest of the flag bright red.

Hudson Taylor Quiz

Color the Chinese tunics whose facts are correct.
Draw a big X over the ones whose facts are incorrect.

Blond-haired Hudson was told he would fit in perfectly in China.

Hudson studied to be a doctor before he went to China.

Hudson enjoyed as many comforts as he could before he left for China.

Hudson formed a group called China Inland Mission.

Hudson and his team refused to dress like the Chinese to fit in.

Hudson used his skill as a doctor to help heal many of the Chinese.

A kind innkeeper in Yangchow made Hudson and his team feel welcome.

The educated Chinese leaders of Yangchow liked Hudson and his team.

Hudson and his team helped the sick and shared their food with the Chinese.

Hudson accomplished so much in China because he did everything himself.

Fun with Rhyme

It's your turn to be a poet. See if you can fill in the correct word inside each Chinese tunic without looking at your book on Hudson Taylor. Hint: The word rhymes with the last word in the second line.

Word Bank

shoes
you
stay
nose
team

The missionary shook his head,
    and said, "You'll never do.
Your blue eyes and blond hair will make
    the Chinese run from

And so they put on Chinese suits,
    pajama-like and blue,
and then to fit in even better
    added curled-up

When Hudson ate a meal with chopsticks,
    many Chinese chose
to peer at his blue eyes and touch
    his long and bumpy

It wasn't long before the poor
    were coming every day.
The missionaries fed them and
    encouraged them to

And once they'd found a house for rent,
    there was a constant stream
of Chinese who were curious
    to meet this foreign

Hudson Taylor Crossword Puzzle

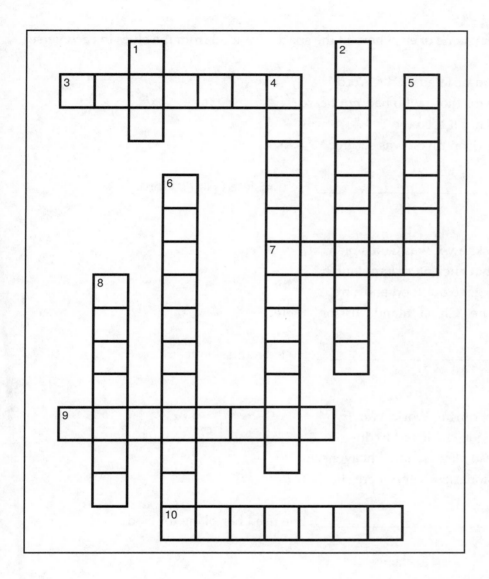

Word Bank

chopsticks

Buddha

England

China

tuberculosis

drought

merchandise

pigtail

mandarin

wok

Across

3. A long period with little or no rain.
7. Country where Hudson became a missionary.
9. An important person of authority in China.
10. Country in Britain where Hudson grew up.

Down

1. A metal pan used for Oriental cooking.
2. What Chinese use to eat with.
4. The disease that Hudson got overseas.
5. The god the Chinese worshiped.
6. Goods that can be bought or sold.
8. Something Hudson wove into his hair.

Can You Name the Hero?

See if you can write the correct name of each hero in the space provided from the clues in each verse.

Can you name the hero who translated God's Word
   in the Burmese language for those who had not heard?
Can you name the hero who hid it secretly
   inside a pillow while in prison till he was set free?

   His name was _____. He translated God's Word.

Can you name the hero who knew it was God's plan
   for him to go to China, that ancient, distant land?
Can you name the hero who gave out food and care
   with a group he named the "China Inland Mission" there?

   His name was _____. He led a mission team.

Can you name the hero who, during World War Two,
   became a woman pilot, a job she loved to do?
Can you name the hero whose plane seemed heavensent
   by bringing help to missionaries everywhere she went?

   Her name was _____. She used her plane for God.

Can you name the hero who learned a doctor's skill
   so he could go to Africa and heal those who were ill?
Can you name the hero who traveled tribal land,
   going places unexplored to serve as God's own hands?

   His name was _____. He served as God's own hands.

Note: This exercise can also be sung by following along on the companion CD for books 9–12. When the chorus is repeated the second time, the answers are included.

Answers to "Can You Name the Hero?"

1. Adoniram Judson

2. Hudson Taylor

3. Betty Greene

4. David Livingstone

Answers to Questions

Answers to Betty Greene

Betty Greene Quiz: Correct Facts

❖ Betty learned how to fly a large float plane near her home.
❖ Betty started a flying ministry after the war.
❖ Betty delivered food, mail, and medical supplies to the missionaries.
❖ Betty flew a red biplane into Mexico.
❖ Betty flew into an unexplored island called New Guinea.
❖ God wants us to use our gifts for Him.

Fun with Rhyme

1. dream
2. best
3. face
4. day
5. sight

Crossword

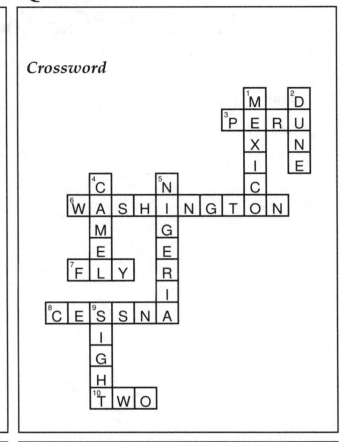

Answers to David Livingstone

David Livingstone Quiz: Correct Facts

❖ David worked in a cotton mill when he was twelve.
❖ David became a doctor because they were needed overseas.
❖ David gave the chief a Bible, and he later became a Christian.
❖ The Africans lived in round huts with roofs of straw.
❖ David encouraged the Africans to talk about their beliefs.
❖ David helped heal a chief whose eyes were damaged.

Fun with Rhyme

1. pants
2. day
3. well
4. ground
5. lands

Crossword

Answers to Adoniram Judson

Adoniram Judson Quiz: Correct Facts

❖ Adoniram attended navigation school when he was young.
❖ In Bible school, Adoniram finally decided that the Bible is true.
❖ After Bible school, Adoniram and his wife left for Burma.
❖ Burmese Christians could not always worship freely but had to meet in secret.
❖ Adoniram hid his translation work in a dirty pillow while he was in prison.

Fun with Rhyme

1. glad
2. do
3. show
4. ground
5. tears

Crossword

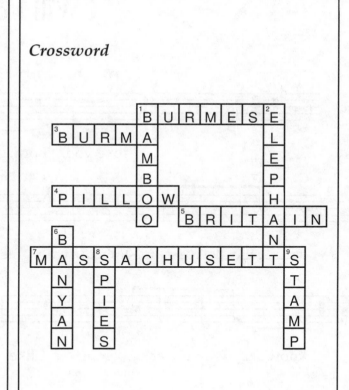

Answers to Hudson Taylor

Hudson Taylor Quiz: Correct Facts

❖ Hudson studied to be a doctor before he went to China.
❖ Hudson formed a group called China Inland Mission.
❖ Hudson used his skill as a doctor to help heal many of the Chinese.
❖ A kind innkeeper in Yangchow made Hudson and his team feel welcome.
❖ Hudson and his team helped the sick and shared their food with the Chinese.

Fun with Rhyme

1. you
2. shoes
3. nose
4. stay
5. team

Crossword

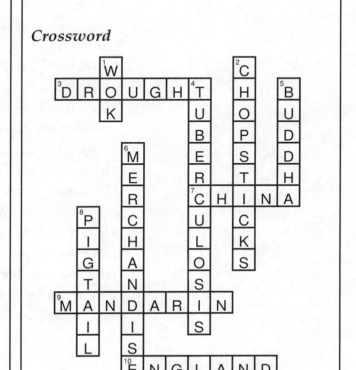

I Will Follow

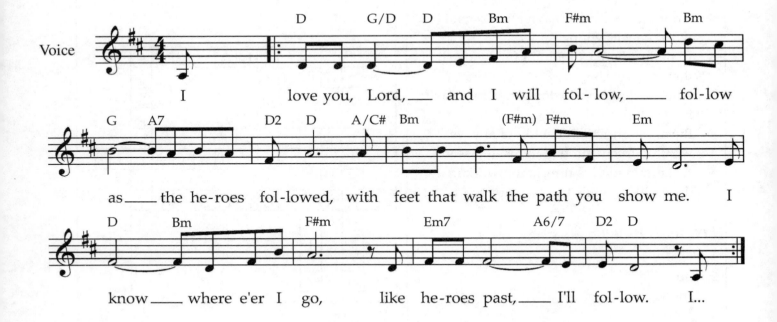

I love you, Lord,___ and I will fol- low,_____ fol-low
as___ the he-roes fol-lowed, with feet that walk the path you show me.   I
know___ where e'er I go,   like he-roes past,___ I'll fol-low.   I...

2. I love You, Lord, and I will follow,
   follow as the heroes followed,
   with hands that help in ways You guide me.
   I know where e'er I go,
   like heroes past, I'll follow.

3. I love You, Lord, and I will follow,
   follow as the heroes followed,
   with ears that hear the truth You tell me.
   I know where e'er I go,
   like heroes past, I'll follow.

4. I love You, Lord, and I will follow,
   follow as the heroes followed,
   with eyes that see the needs around me.
   I know where e'er I go,
   like heroes past, I'll follow.

Syllabus

Week 1

Betty Greene: 30-minute Class

1. Read the book *Betty Greene: Flying High*. Tell the children to listen carefully because there will be a short quiz afterward (10 minutes).
2. Take the Betty Greene Quiz on page 19 (5 minutes).
3. Learn and sing the "Betty Greene Song" by listening to the companion CD and following along on page 9 (5 minutes).
4. Do the Shoebox Activity on page 15 (10 minutes).

Betty Greene: 45-minute Class

1. Read the book *Betty Greene: Flying High*. Tell the children to listen carefully because there will be a short quiz afterward (10 minutes).
2. Take the Betty Greene Quiz on page 19 (5 minutes).
3. Do Fun with Rhyme on page 20 (5 minutes).
4. Learn and sing the "Betty Greene Song" by listening to the companion CD and following along on page 9 (5 minutes).
5. Color the Map on page 17 (5 minutes).
6. Do the Shoebox Activity on page 15 (10 minutes).
7. Sing the Character Song "We'll Try Hard to Serve" by listening to the companion CD and following along on page 13 (5 minutes).

Week 2

Betty Greene: 30-minute Class

1. Review the "Betty Greene Song" on page 9 (5 minutes).
2. Color the Map on page 17 (5 minutes).
3. Learn about the Good Character Quality of Betty on pages 10–12 (15 minutes) and sing the Character Song "We'll Try Hard to Serve" on page 13 (5 minutes).

Betty Greene: 45-minute Class

1. Review the "Betty Greene Song" on page 9 (5 minutes).
2. Learn about the Good Character Quality of Betty on pages 10–12 (15 minutes) and sing the Character Song "We'll Try Hard to Serve" on page 13 (5 minutes).
3. Learn about and color the Echidna Spiny Anteater of New Guinea on page 16 (10 minutes).

4. Color the flag of New Guinea on page 18 (10 minutes).

Optional: While the children are coloring, play the "Betty Greene Song," "We'll Try Hard to Serve," and "I Will Follow" from the companion CD for them to listen to.

Week 3

David Livingstone: 30-minute Class

1. Read the book *David Livingstone: Courageous Explorer*. Tell them to listen carefully because there will be a short quiz afterward (10 minutes).
2. Take the David Livingstone Quiz on page 37 (5 minutes).
3. Learn and sing the "David Livingstone Song" by listening to the companion CD and following along on page 25 (5 minutes).
4. Do the Shoebox Activity on page 32 (10 minutes).

David Livingstone: 45-minute Class

1. Read the book *David Livingstone: Courageous Explorer*. Tell them to listen carefully because there will be a short quiz afterward (10 minutes).
2. Take the David Livingstone Quiz on page 37 (5 minutes).
3. Learn and sing the "David Livingstone Song" by listening to the companion CD and following along on page 25 (5 minutes).
4. Learn about the Good Character Quality of David on pages 26–28 (10 minutes) and sing the Character Song "We Will Be So Bold" on page 29 (5 minutes).
5. Do the Character Activity on pages 30 and 31 (5 minutes).
6. Review the Character Song "We Will Be So Bold" on page 29 (5 minutes).

Week 4

David Livingstone: 30-minute Class

1. Learn about the Good Character Quality of David on pages 26–28 (10 minutes) and sing the Character Song "We Will Be So Bold" on page 29 (5 minutes).
2. Do the Character Activity on pages 30 and 31 (5 minutes).
3. Color the David Livingstone picture on page 23 (10 minutes).
Optional: While the children are coloring, play the "David Livingstone Song," "We Will Be So Bold," and "I Will Follow" from the companion CD for them to listen to.

David Livingstone: 45-minute Class

1. Review the "David Livingstone Song" on page 25 (5 minutes).
2. Do Fun with Rhyme on page 38 (5 minutes).

3. Learn about and make Africa's Lions on pages 33 and 34 (20 minutes).
4. Review the Character Song "We Will Be So Bold" on page 29 (5 minutes).
5. Color the map and flag of Scotland on pages 35 and 36 (10 minutes).
   Optional: While the children are coloring, play the "David Livingstone Song" and the Prayer Song "I Will Follow" from the companion CD for them to listen to.

Week 5

Adoniram Judson: 30-minute Class

1. Read the book *Adoniram Judson: A Grand Purpose* (10 minutes).
2. Learn and sing the "Adoniram Judson Song" by listening to the companion CD and following along on page 43 (5 minutes).
3. Do the Character Activity on pages 48 and 49 (5 minutes).
4. Do the Shoebox Activity on page 50 (10 minutes).

Adoniram Judson: 45-minute Class

1. Read the book *Adoniram Judson: A Grand Purpose*. Tell the children to listen carefully because there will be a short quiz afterward (10 minutes).
2. Take the Adoniram Judson Quiz on page 55 (5 minutes).
3. Learn and sing the "Adoniram Judson Song" by listening to the companion CD and following along on page 43 (5 minutes).
4. Do the Character Activity on pages 48 and 49 (5 minutes).
5. Do the Shoebox Activity on page 50 (10 minutes).
6. Learn and sing the Character Song "We'll Be Purposeful" on page 47 (5 minutes).
7. Sing the Prayer Song "I Will Follow" on page 78 (5 minutes).

Week 6

Adoniram Judson: 30-minute Class

1. Review the "Adoniram Judson Song" on page 43 (5 minutes).
2. Learn about the Good Character Quality of Adoniram on pages 44–46 (10 minutes) and sing the Character Song "We'll Be Purposeful" on page 47 (5 minutes).
3. Learn about and color the Bengal Tiger of Burma on pages 51 and 52 (10 minutes).
   Optional: While the children are coloring, play the "Adoniram Judson Song," "We'll Be Purposeful," and "I Will Follow" from the companion CD for them to listen to.

Adoniram Judson: 45-minute Class

1. Review the "Adoniram Judson Song" on page 43 (5 minutes).
2. Do Fun with Rhyme on page 56 (5 minutes).

3. Learn about the Good Character Quality of Adoniram on pages 44–46 (10 minutes) and sing the Character Song "We'll Be Purposeful" on page 47 (5 minutes).

4. Learn about and color the Bengal Tiger of Burma on pages 51 and 52 (10 minutes).
   Optional: While the children are coloring, play the "Adoniram Judson Song," "We'll Be Purposeful," and "I Will Follow" from the companion CD for them to listen to.

5. Review the Character Song "We'll Be Purposeful" on page 57 (5 minutes).

6. Review the Prayer Song "I Will Follow" on page 78 (5 minutes).

Week 7

Hudson Taylor: 30-minute Class

1. Read the book *Hudson Taylor: Friend of China* (10 minutes).
2. Do the Shoebox Activity on page 67 (20 minutes).

Hudson Taylor: 45-minute Class

1. Read the book *Hudson Taylor: Friend of China*. Tell the children to listen carefully because there will be a short quiz afterward (10 minutes).
2. Take the Hudson Taylor Quiz on page 71 (5 minutes).
3. Learn and sing the "Hudson Taylor Song" by listening to the companion CD and following along on page 61 (5 minutes).
4. Do the Shoebox Activity on page 67 (20 minutes).
5. Learn and sing the "Can You Name the Hero?" song by listening to the companion CD and following along on page 74 (5 minutes).

Week 8

Hudson Taylor: 30-minute Class

1. Learn and sing the "Hudson Taylor Song" on page 61 (5 minutes).
2. Learn about the Good Character Quality of Hudson on pages 62–64 (10 minutes) and sing the Character Song "We'll Work Hard to Lead" on page 65 (5 minutes).
3. Do the Character Activity on page 66 (10 minutes).

Hudson Taylor: 45-minute Class

1. Review the "Can You Name the Hero?" song on page 74 (5 minutes).
2. Review the "Hudson Taylor Song" on page 61 (5 minutes).
3. Learn about the Good Character Quality of Hudson on pages 62–64 (10 minutes) and sing the Character Song "We'll Work Hard to Lead" on page 65 (5 minutes).
4. Do the Character Activity on page 66 (10 minutes).
5. Review the Character Song "We'll Work Hard to Lead" on page 65 (5 minutes).

6. Color the map and flag of China on pages 69 and 70 (5 minutes).

   Optional: While the children are coloring, play the "Hudson Taylor Song," "We'll Work Hard to Lead," and "I Will Follow" from the companion CD for them to listen to.

Week 9

Betty Greene: 30-minute class

1. Reread the book *Betty Greene: Flying High* (10 minutes).
2. Do the Character Activity for Betty on page 14 (15 minutes).
3. Color the Betty Greene picture on page 7 (5 minutes).

   Optional: While the children are coloring, play the "Betty Greene Song," "We'll Try Hard to Serve," and "I Will Follow" from the companion CD for them to listen to.

Betty Greene: 45-minute class

1. Reread the book *Betty Greene: Flying High*. Tell them to listen carefully because there will be a crossword puzzle afterward (10 minutes).
2. Work the Crossword Puzzle on page 21 (10 minutes).

   Please note: For very young children, sing the "Betty Greene Song" on page 9, the Character Song "We'll Try Hard to Serve" on page 13, and "I Will Follow" on page 78 instead of working the crossword puzzle.
3. Do the Character Activity for Betty on page 14 (15 minutes).
4. Color the Betty Greene picture on page 7 (10 minutes).

   Optional: While the children are coloring, play the "Betty Greene Song," "We'll Try Hard to Serve," and "I Will Follow" from the companion CD for them to listen to.

Week 10

David Livingstone: 30-minute class

1. Reread the book *David Livingstone: Courageous Explorer* (10 minutes).
2. Learn about and make Africa's Lions on pages 33 and 34 (20 minutes).

   Optional: While they are making their lions, play the "David Livingstone Song," "We Will Be So Bold," and "I Will Follow" from the companion CD for them to listen to.

David Livingstone: 45-minute class

1. Reread the book *David Livingstone: Courageous Explorer*. Tell them to listen carefully because there will be a crossword puzzle afterward (10 minutes).
2. Work the Crossword Puzzle on page 39 (10 minutes).

   Please note: For very young children, sing the "David Livingstone Song" on page 25, the Character Song "We Will Be So Bold" on page 29, and "I Will Follow" on page 78 instead of working the crossword puzzle.
3. Do the Shoebox Activity on page 32 (10 minutes).

4. Color the David Livingstone picture on page 23 (10 minutes).
    Optional: While the children are coloring, play the "David Livingstone Song," "We Will Be So Bold," and "I Will Follow" from the companion CD for them to listen to.
5. Review the "David Livingstone" Song on page 25 (5 minutes).

Week 11

Adoniram Judson: 30-minute class

1. Reread the book *Adoniram Judson: A Grand Purpose*. Tell them to listen carefully because there will be a short quiz afterward (10 minutes).
2. Take the Adoniram Judson Quiz on page 55 (5 minutes).
3. Review the "Adoniram Judson Song" on page 43 (5 minutes).
4. Color the Adoniram Judson picture on page 41 (10 minutes).
    Optional: While the children are coloring, play the "Adoniram Judson Song," "We'll Be Purposeful," and "I Will Follow" from the companion CD for them to listen to.

Adoniram Judson: 45-minute class

1. Reread the book *Adoniram Judson: A Grand Purpose*. Tell them to listen carefully because there will be a crossword puzzle afterward (10 minutes).
2. Work the Crossword Puzzle on page 57 (10 minutes).
    Please note: For very young children, sing the "Adoniram Judson Song" on page 43, "We'll Be Purposeful" on page 47, and "I Will Follow" on page 78 instead of working the crossword puzzle.
3. Color the flag of Burma on page 54 (10 minutes).
4. Color the Adoniram Judson picture on page 41 (10 minutes).
    Optional: While the children are coloring, play the "Adoniram Judson Song," "We'll Be Purposeful," and "I Will Follow" from the companion CD for them to listen to.
5. Review the Prayer Song "I Will Follow" on page 78 (5 minutes).

Week 12

Hudson Taylor: 30-minute class

1. Reread the book *Hudson Taylor: Friend of China*. Tell the children to listen carefully because there will be a short quiz afterward (10 minutes).
2. Take the Hudson Taylor Quiz on page 71 (5 minutes).
3. Review the "Hudson Taylor Song" on page 61 (5 minutes).
4. Color the Hudson Taylor picture on page 59 (10 minutes).
    Optional: While the children are coloring, play the "Hudson Taylor Song," "We'll Work Hard to Lead," and "I Will Follow" from the companion CD for them to listen to.

Hudson Taylor: 45-minute class

1. Reread the book *Hudson Taylor: Friend of China*. Tell them to listen carefully because there will be a crossword puzzle afterward (10 minutes).
2. Work the Crossword Puzzle on page 73 (10 minutes).
   Please note: For very young children, sing the "Hudson Taylor Song" on page 61, the Character Song "We'll Work Hard to Lead" on page 65, and "I Will Follow" on page 78 instead of working the crossword puzzle.
3. Make the Chinese lanterns on page 68 (15 minutes).
4. Color the Hudson Taylor picture on page 59 (10 minutes).
   Optional: While the children are coloring, play the "Hudson Taylor Song," "We'll Work Hard to Lead," and "I Will Follow" from the companion CD for them to listen to.

Week 13

30-minute Class

1. Sing the "Can You Name the Hero?" song by listening to the companion CD and following along on page 74 (5 minutes).
2. Read the definitions of the character traits on each of the Good Character Quality pages and see if the children can guess the trait and the name of the hero that the trait applies to (5 minutes).
3. Play the game "Who Am I?" Have each child pick the name of one of the four heroes from a basket and give a clue about who that hero is. Let the rest of the class try to guess who the hero is (10 minutes).
4. Have each child pick the name of one of the four heroes from a basket and draw a picture that makes others think of that hero, e.g., a plane, Bible, or lion (10 minutes).

45-minute Class

1. Sing the "Can You Name the Hero?" song by listening to the companion CD and following along on page 74 (5 minutes).
2. Read the definitions of the character traits on each of the Good Character Quality pages and see if the children can guess the trait and the name of the hero that the trait applies to (5 minutes).
3. Play the game "Who Am I?" Have each child pick the name of one of the four heroes from a basket and give a clue about who that hero is. Let the rest of the class try to guess who the hero is (10 minutes).
4. Have each child pick the name of one of the four heroes from a basket and draw a picture that makes others think of that hero, e.g., a plane, Bible, or lion (10 minutes).
5. Tell who your favorite hero is and why (5 minutes).
6. Ask the children to pick their favorite songs and sing them (10 minutes).

Notes

Heroes for Young Readers

Written by Renee Taft Meloche • Illustrated by Bryan Pollard

Don't miss the exciting stories of other Christian heroes! Whether reading for themselves or being read to, children love the captivating rhyming text and unforgettable color illustrations of the Heroes for Young Readers series. See the next page for more activity guides and CDs.

BOOKS 1–4

Gladys Aylward: Daring to Trust • Trust in God enabled Gladys Aylward (1902–1970) to safely lead nearly one hundred Chinese orphans on a daring journey that saved their lives. ISBN 1-57658-228-0

Nate Saint: Heavenbound • Nate Saint (1923–1956) flew his plane over the jungles of Ecuador, helping missionaries reach isolated Indians with God's great love. ISBN 1-57658-229-9

Eric Liddell: Running for a Higher Prize • From winning Olympic gold as a runner to leaving his fame in Scotland behind to go to China as a missionary, Eric Liddell (1902–1945) put God in first place. ISBN 1-57658-230-2

George Müller: Faith to Feed Ten Thousand • George Müller (1805–1898) opened an orphanage, trusting God to faithfully provide for the needs of thousands of England's orphaned children. ISBN 1-57658-232-9

BOOKS 5–8

Corrie ten Boom: Shining in the Darkness • Corrie ten Boom (1892–1983) and her family risked everything to extend God's hand of love and protection to their Jewish neighbors during WWII. ISBN 1-57658-231-0

Amy Carmichael: Rescuing the Children • Amy Carmichael (1867–1951) rescued hundreds of women and children, first in Irish slums and then in India, by fearing God and nothing else. ISBN 1-57658-233-7

Mary Slessor: Courage in Africa • Mary Slessor (1848–1915) courageously shared Jesus' life and freedom with the unreached tribes of Africa's Calabar region. ISBN 1-57658-237-X

William Carey: Bearer of Good News • William Carey (1761–1834) left England behind and sailed to faraway India, where he devoted himself to translating the Bible into the native languages. ISBN 1-57658-236-1

BOOKS 9–12

Hudson Taylor: Friend of China • Known as one of the greatest pioneer missionaries of all time, Hudson Taylor (1832–1905) overcame huge obstacles to reach the Chinese. ISBN 1-57658-234-5

David Livingstone: Courageous Explorer • Trailblazing explorer David Livingstone (1813–1873) would not let anything stand in his way as he mapped unexplored Africa and healed the sick. ISBN 1-57658-238-8

Adoniram Judson: A Grand Purpose • Even imprisonment could not stop America's first foreign missionary, Adoniram Judson (1788–1850), as he translated the Bible into Burmese. ISBN 1-57658-240-X

Betty Greene: Flying High • Betty Greene (1920–1997) combined her love of flying with her love for Christ by helping found the Mission Aviation Fellowship. ISBN 1-57658-239-6

BOOKS 13–16

Lottie Moon: A Generous Offering • As a missionary to some of the poorest cities in China, once-wealthy Lottie Moon (1840–1912) experienced having nothing to eat. In dire circumstances, Lottie's first priority was teaching others about God's love. ISBN 1-57658-243-4

Jim Elliot: A Light for God • Jim Elliot (1927–1956) bravely faced both the wonders and the dangers of the South American jungle to share God's love with the feared and isolated Auca people. ISBN 1-57658-235-3

Jonathan Goforth: Never Give Up • In faraway China, despite danger and ridicule, Jonathan Goforth (1859–1936) and his wife generously opened their home to thousands of Chinese visitors, sharing the Good News of the gospel. ISBN 1-57658-242-6

Cameron Townsend: Planting God's Word • After planting God's Word in the hearts of people all over Guatemala and Mexico, Cameron Townsend (1896–1982) started Wycliffe Bible Translators so that all people could read the Good News for themselves. ISBN 1-57658-241-8

For a free catalog of books and materials contact
YWAM Publishing, P.O. Box 55787, Seattle, WA 98155
1-800-922-2143, www.ywampublishing.com

Heroes for Young Readers Activity Guides and CDs
by Renee Taft Meloche

Whether for home, school, or Sunday school, don't miss these fun-filled activity guides and CDs presenting the lives of other Heroes for Young Readers.

Heroes for Young Readers Activity Guides
For Books 1–4: Gladys Aylward, Nate Saint, Eric Liddell, George Müller • 1-57658-367-8
For Books 5–8: Amy Carmichael, Corrie ten Boom, Mary Slessor, William Carey • 1-57658-368-6
For Books 9–12: Betty Greene, David Livingstone, Adoniram Judson, Hudson Taylor • 1-57658-369-4

Heroes for Young Readers Activity Audio CD
Each activity guide has an available audio CD with book readings, songs, and fun activity tracks, helping you to get the most out of the Activity Guides!

CD for Books 1–4 • 1-57658-396-1
CD for Books 5–8 • 1-57658-397-X
CD for Books 9–12 • 1-57658-398-8

Heroes for Young Readers Activity Guide Package Special
Includes the activity guide, audio CD, and four corresponding Heroes for Young Readers hardcover books.

For Books 1–4 Package • 1-57658-375-9
For Books 5–8 Package • 1-57658-376-7
For Books 9–12 Package • 1-57658-377-5

Christian Heroes: Then & Now
by Janet and Geoff Benge

The Heroes for Young Readers books are based on the Christian Heroes: Then & Now biographies by Janet and Geoff Benge. Discover these exciting, true adventures for ages ten and up! Many unit study curriculum guides for older students are also available to accompany these biographies.

Gladys Aylward: The Adventure of a Lifetime • 1-57658-019-9
Nate Saint: On a Wing and a Prayer • 1-57658-017-2
Hudson Taylor: Deep in the Heart of China • 1-57658-016-4
Amy Carmichael: Rescuer of Precious Gems • 1-57658-018-0
Eric Liddell: Something Greater Than Gold • 1-57658-137-3
Corrie ten Boom: Keeper of the Angels' Den • 1-57658-136-5
William Carey: Obliged to Go • 1-57658-147-0
George Müller: The Guardian of Bristol's Orphans • 1-57658-145-4
Jim Elliot: One Great Purpose • 1-57658-146-2
Mary Slessor: Forward into Calabar • 1-57658-148-9
David Livingstone: Africa's Trailblazer • 1-57658-153-5
Betty Greene: Wings to Serve • 1-57658-152-7
Adoniram Judson: Bound for Burma • 1-57658-161-6
Cameron Townsend: Good News in Every Language • 1-57658-164-0
Jonathan Goforth: An Open Door in China • 1-57658-174-8
Lottie Moon: Giving Her All for China • 1-57658-188-8
John Williams: Messenger of Peace • 1-57658-256-6
William Booth: Soup, Soap, and Salvation • 1-57658-258-2
Rowland Bingham: Into Africa's Interior • 1-57658-282-5
Ida Scudder: Healing Bodies, Touching Hearts • 1-57658-285-X
Wilfred Grenfell: Fisher of Men • 1-57658-292-2
Lillian Trasher: The Greatest Wonder in Egypt • 1-57658-305-8
Loren Cunningham: Into All the World • 1-57658-199-3
Florence Young: Mission Accomplished • 1-57658-313-9
Sundar Singh: Footprints Over the Mountains • 1-57658-318-X
C.T. Studd: No Retreat • 1-57658-288-4

For a free catalog of books and materials contact
YWAM Publishing, P.O. Box 55787, Seattle, WA 98155
1-800-922-2143, www.ywampublishing.com